CONTENTS

INTRODUCTION

In 2012 I was commissioned by Runnymede Borough Council to create an embroidery panel to mark the 800th anniversary of the sealing of Magna Carta. Little did I know, when first commissioned, that this project would grow to twelve panels, and from that would come exhibitions throughout the UK, a book, a website, numerous television, radio and press appearances, or that I would contribute two embroidered pennants to Magna Carta Garden at the 2015 RHS Chelsea Flower Show.

To top it all, I never imaged that I would have the honour of being appointed an Aymeric Dame of the Knights Templar of England for my involvement in Magna Carta 800th Anniversary, or that Derek Taylor, one of the country's leading historians would contribute to this book.

The twelve panels were all designed and hand embroidered by myself and a team of twelve volunteers. We have spent nearly 30,000 hours of our time to create the panels and the project is now completed.

This book is the story behind the panels, with detailed pictures and descriptions of each panel.

The panels illustrate the events leading up to the sealing of Magna Carta and also how Magna Carta influenced the spread of law and order throughout former British colonies and commonwealth countries.

The Magna Carta Embroideries are being displayed throughout the UK, as part of The Magna Carta 800th anniversary events, with the aim of creating a lasting legacy to honour one of the most important historical events in British history.

As a tribute to a remarkable document, I hope that The Magna Carta Embroideries will be a legacy to the country, to be viewed and enjoyed by as many people as possible over the coming years.

Rhoda Nevins

ABOUT RHODA NEVINS

Rhoda studied embroidery at the Royal School of Needlework and has been involved in some prestigious projects in the last few years, not least being part of the team that embroidered the Duchess of Cambridge's wedding dress. She has also completed a magnificent piece depicting the skyline of the town of Guildford which was presented to the town in memory of her late husband, a former mayor of Guildford and now hangs in G Live in Guildford.

Rhoda also helped to embroider one of the official Olympic quilts which were gifted to each country competing in the 2012 games. She has recently been presented to the Queen and the Duke of Edinburgh on a visit to Southwark Cathedral as part of the team that embroidered Jubilee vestments for the Bishop of Southwark and his area Bishops. Rhoda also takes private commissions as well as running a successful soft furnishing business with clients throughout Surrey and London.

When planning and creating the embroidery and to ensure historical accuracy Rhoda spent a lot of time doing extensive research. Never did she imagine that her O-level history topic on the British Empire and Commonwealth would come in useful fifty years later.

Once work got underway, Rhoda gathered together a team of dedicated and talented group of volunteers, some she had worked with on the Guildford Embroidery, that famous wedding dress and the commemorative quilts for the 2012 Olympics.

The team met monthly and decided which part of the panel they would work on and then bring it back the following month for their embroideries to be appliqued to the various panels. Because of the size of the panels, one of the volunteers, Carolynn Stephens was given the job of lying underneath the frame, so she could pass the needle up to the two women putting the panels together. Small in stature, Carolynn spent many hours lying on the floor, often kept company by one or Rhoda's two cats, while she passed the needle from bottom to top of the embroidery. The broderers on top, had to put a pin through the embroidery to show Carolynn where to return the needle, luckily she wears glasses otherwise it could have been quite dangerous.

A year into the project and Rhoda realised that this was bigger than she could ever imagine. The chair of The Magna Carta Trust for Bury St Edmunds, told her that this was not "just any old embroidery - you are doing this for the nation".

In total the team worked between 20,000 to 30,000 hours, to create the panels and the reaction and feedback has been incredible. There has been a lot of interest from around the world and Rhoda along with the panels has featured in numerous newspapers, magazines and on television and radio.

It would have been impossible for Rhoda to complete this without the dedication and hard work of the team of volunteers who have bought their incredible skills, creativity and dedication to this project, often giving up family time, including weekends and evenings to complete the work.

STORY OF
THE EMBRODERIES

In the historical tradition of telling stories through pictures and embroideries, the embroidered panels explain the events leading up to the sealing of Magna Carta, made under oath and certainly under duress, by King John. Magna Carta sets out the basic rights and freedoms of common people, including the right to trial by jury.

For the first time absolute power was taken from the monarchy and given to the barons, taking the first steps towards the democratic and legal system, upon which our country is founded.

There are only four surviving copies of Magna Carta in the UK, they are in Lincoln and Salisbury Cathedrals and two in the British Library.

The embroidered panels of the charter towns, which include Runnymede, Bury St Edmunds, St Albans, the City of London, Canterbury and Hereford; explain how the barons, supported by the Archbishop of Canterbury, Stephen Langton, overcame the absolute rule of the monarchy and forced King John to seal Magna Carta, with the final version sealed in the City of London by Edward I in 1297.

The international panels, United States of America, Canada, Australia, India and South Africa, tell the story of how the British arrived in the various countries and how and why they left. The panels tell how the principles of Magna Carta, which underpinned British rule in those colonies, influenced the founding, of those independent states and the spread of law and order throughout these countries.

The twelfth panel is of the shields of the 25 barons who were present at the sealing.

The twelve panels are all A1 in size. Their backing material is of heavy weight silk, with appliqué and surface embroidery, using silk and gold threads and all are framed to museum and conservation standard.

The embroideries also have an added element of 3D, to help bring depth to the story and the images they depict, using a variety of materials including silk and gold threads which features on all of the panels.

About the embroideries of King John

King John looks different in each embroidery, because different members of the team have interpreted him in different ways. Rhoda and her team worked on separate elements and then came together once a month, in order for the embroideries to be appliquéd onto the background silk. Everyone has a different style and that is why King John and sometimes other images look different, although overall, it looks as if one person has embroidered all twelve panels. It all adds to creating a unique style, that pays tribute to all the different embroiderer's skills who worked on the project.

TRADITION
OF EMBROIDERY

As an art form, embroidery has been with us since the 5th century BC. Through the centuries, and around the world, embroidery has remained a popular and skilled technique, though it was not until the Industrial Revolution and the development of machinery, that embroidery on a mass scale was possible.

Even with the development of machinery, the popularity and skill of embroidery by hand, continues to this day throughout the world.

With techniques such as gold work, stump work, fine white work, crewel work and silk shading which are the main skills embroiderers learn.

It has taken Rhoda about 12 years to learn all the different techniques and to refine her skill and ability, to reach the standard she is at today. It has taken hours of dedicated practise and commitment, to be able to embroider to this level.

The Magna Carta Embroidery project, is a testament to the skills and talents of the team who have created such a beautifully designed, detailed and intricate project. It is interesting that some of the skills and stitches used in these panels, would have been used in a crude form in 1215, although stump work and crewel work did not come in until the Tudor times. Embroidery really started to take off as an art form, when Catherine of Aragon brought black work from Spain, a form of embroidery, just using black threads on a white fabric for clothing. It was used to decorate collars and cuffs.

MAGNA CARTA: CHAMPION OF LIBERTY

Back in 1215, Magna Carta was like many a new-born in the Middle Ages: the odds were stacked against its survival. It was a sickly baby with abusive parents. Those who'd conceived it - King John and the barons – abandoned it within three months, and the Pope even declared it dead.

Magna Carta itself looked ill-equipped for a long and healthy life. Most of its 63 clauses were peppered with feudal jargon - 'trithings', 'halberget', hardly words to echo down the ages. And, it contains no resounding statement such as, 'We are all equal under the law.'

So why do we rightly celebrate Magna Carta's 800th birthday? Well, it wasn't an entirely poorly child. It had a sturdy heart that would help it live on. The Great Charter showed that even a king must obey the law, and specifically, that arbitrary punishment is wrong.

Magna Carta however wasn't finished there. It was – and still is – a living being. Over the centuries, whenever a king faced revolt, he'd be forced to make concessions. And these were often incorporated into an updated Magna Carta, which more and more established the rights of ordinary folk.

Then, during the mighty clash between crown and parliament in the seventeenth century, the opposition needed evidence of biblical proportions to combat the king's claim that he had absolute power given him by God. The great jurist, Sir Edward Coke turned to Magna Carta.

It was his commentary on the Great Charter that became the inspiration for those fighting for freedom and justice, not only in England but elsewhere in the world. Magna Carta became the foundation of the American Bill of Rights, and the constitutions of Canada, Australia and India.

It's been called 'England's greatest export.' Wherever in the world today, there is injustice and tyranny, you may hear protesters voice two Medieval Latin words that will forever be England's glory: Magna Carta!

Derek Taylor

THE RUNNYMEDE PANEL

The Runnymede panel features King John's crest in the middle, an embroidery of Stephen Langton, The Archbishop of Canterbury on the left and King John on the right.

Stephen Langton who was Archbishop of Canterbury between 1207 and his death in 1228 worked with the barons to end King John's absolute rule. The dispute between King John and the Pope over his election was a major factor in ensuring that the barons had the support of Rome leading up to Magna Carta.

The panel shows the barons, in their various colours, on their way to Runnymede to ensure the document was sealed, so that they could assert their power of the king.

In those days, there were only a few colours available and so heraldic shields used shapes to impart meaning and to signify a different family name, creating a language of their own. For example a horizontal or diagonal stripe in a different colour meant 'the son of a baron'.

Runnymede is seen by many, to be the birthplace of democracy and despite it being no more than an open meadow, this land holds enormous significance for people all over the world.

RUNNYMEDE

Stephen Langton
Archbishop of Canterbury

King John
of England

The Sealing of the Magna Carta
15th June 1215

THE CANTERBURY PANEL

For many people the story of how Magna Carta came into being starts in Canterbury.

The Canterbury panel shows people travelling along the Pilgrims Way to Canterbury Cathedral to honour the memory of the Archbishop of Canterbury, Thomas Beckett who was murdered in Canterbury Cathedral on 29 December 1170 by four knights who were followers of King Henry II, who was John's father.

In 1170, Canterbury became a focus for change after Thomas Beckett's execution, as he was considered the most holy man in the country and the execution angered Pope Innocent III (1198 to 1216) who was determined to get revenge.

The panel shows monks scribing Magna Carta and Stephen Langdon, the Archbishop of Canterbury, the Pope's representative in England in 1215 and the main force in getting Magna Carta sealed. The Catholic Church claimed supremacy over King John, empowering Stephen Langton to gather the support of the barons, to bring about the changes that led to the sealing of Magna Carta.

CANTERBURY

Saint Thomas Becket

Scribing the
Magna Carta

Pope Innocent III

Stephan Langton
Archbishop of Canterbury
with King John

THE BURY ST EDMUNDS PANEL

The Bury St Edmunds panel was specially commissioned by the Bury St Edmunds Magna Carta Trust.

The Bury St Edmunds panel features St Edmund who legend has it, was tied to a tree and shot with arrows and then decapitated, after he refused the demands of the invading Danes to renounce Christ. The rest of the panel features some of the main buildings that played a part in Bury's role in Magna Carta, they include Abbey Gateway, Moyse's Hall Museum, The Guildhall and the Norman Tower. The panel also features a group of barons, which in 1214 met in the Abbey Church to swear an oath to compel King John to accept the Charter of Liberties, a direct precursor to Magna Carta.

At the bottom of the panel the Borough's motto 'Sacrarium Regis, Cunabula Legis' or 'Shrine of a King, Cradle of the Law' also reflects the town's role in this significant historical event.

BURY ST EDMUNDS

Sacrarium Regis Cunabula Legis
Shrine of a King Cradle of the Law

THE CITY OF LONDON PANEL

The City of London played an active role in the events that led to Magna Carta's creation in 1215 although the London Magna Carta was not sealed until 1297.

By 1297 the original charter had gone through a number of iterations. London is the only city specifically named in Magna Carta and the clause that states; "the City of London shall have all its ancient liberties by land as well as by water", is embroidered at the bottom of the panel.

Featured on the panel is the shield of William de Hardell, Mayor of London and one of the Enforcers of Magna Carta.

Also featured is the Shield of Robert Fitzwalter, who was one of the most powerful and wealthiest men in the country. He was Sheriff of London and leader of the baronial uprising against King John and an Enforcer of Magna Carta.

The iconic City of London crest, which first appeared in a crude form in 1539 features on the embroidery and taking centre stage in the panel is Edward I seen here sealing the 1297 Magna Carta surrounded by the barons.

Two of London's gates Moor Gate and Spitalfields Gate are on the panel and Moor Gate is seen here being guarded by one of the Knights Templar.

Temple Church also features on the embroidery and there have been Knights Templar in London since 1100. As a tribute to their crucial role in Magna Carta, we have featured two Aymeric Medals created for the 800th anniversary and kindly donated by the KnightsTemplar.

CITY OF LONDON

William de Hardell
Mayor of London

Robert Fitzwalter

CITY OF LONDON

Edward I of England

Moore - Gate

Sheriff of London

Spitalfield Gate

Temple Church

Edward I Sealing the
1297 Magna Carta

Knights Templar

The City of London shall enjoy all its ancient liberties and
free customs, both by land and by water.

THE ST ALBANS PANEL

The St Albans panel explains the crucial role played by the Charter Town in the creation of Magna Carta.

Churchmen and barons, led by Stephen Langton, the Archbishop of Canterbury, held their first meeting in St Albans to discuss their grievances against King John.

In 1213 this historic meeting eventually led to the articles that became Magna Carta, sealed at Runnymede in 1215.

The St Albans panel features the main buildings in St Albans that played a significant part in the gathering together of the barons and Stephen Langton to discuss the formation of Magna Carta. Seen here is the Abbey, and the Clock Tower. There is also an embroidery of a pilgrims badge of St Alban. When pilgrims went on pilgrimages they wanted a souvenir of their trip and so they collected tin badges. There is also the crest of St Albans and St Alban himself carrying a palm leaf symbol.

ST ALBANS

Pilgrim's Badge of
Saint Alban

Saint Alban

King John

THE HEREFORD PANEL

Hereford has one of the four remaining copies of the revised versions of Magna Carta, which was sealed by Henry III in 1217. It is also home to the Mappa Mundi, the oldest existing map of the world, dating from 1285. The Hereford panel version of Magna Carta also features St Ethelbert the King, the patron saint, who was murdered in the 8th Century and at his tomb, it is said that miracles were to have happened.

Hereford Cathedral and the Town Bridge can also be seen on the embroidery, and of course you can also see the Chained Library of Thomas Cantilupe - it is the only library of this type to survive with all the chains, rods and locks still intact.

The panel also shows the Shrine of St Thomas of Hereford.

Apart from the Mappa Mundi, Hereford is most famous for the Charter of the Forest 1216, a charter that was originally sealed in England by the then young King Henry III. A companion document to Magna Carta and many of its provisions were in force for centuries afterwards. Finally the panel shows the Civil War 1215-1216, the year that followed the sealing of the original Magna Carta which saw almost constant war.

HEREFORD

St Ethelbert the King

Chained Library

Mappa Mundi

The Shrine of
Thomas Cantilupe

Civil War
July 1215 - October 1216

Charter of
the Forest 1217

Magna Carta Third Writ 1217

THE BARONS' SHIELDS

This panel features the shields of the twenty-five feudal barons who came together to force King John to accept Magna Carta. They did this to limit his powers by law and protect their rights. This meant that the King was now a subject and no longer above the law.

One of the main reasons many of the barons joined the rebellion in 1215, was as a protest against the extortionate levies they were required to pay to the king for their extensive land holdings that had been granted to them by the crown. In addition to land taxes, they also paid the king further levies to get out of military service.

The reason that there were 25 barons was to avoid any chance of a voting split.

In the embroidery you can see each baron's names; some who make up some of the country's oldest surviving families.

MAGNA CARTA BARONS 1215

William de Hardell

William Marshall

Richard de Montfitchet

Robert de Vere

John FitzRobert

Roger Bigod

William Mallet

John de Lacy

Robert de Ros

Robert Fitzwalter

Geoffrey de Say

Hugh Bigod

Saher de Quincy

Geoffrey de Mandeville

Eustace de Vesci

William de Mowbray

Richard de Clare

Henry de Bohun

Richard de Percy

William d'Aubigney

William de Lanvellei

Roger de Montbegan

Guilbert de Clare

William de Forz

William de Huntingfield

THE AMERICA PANEL

Magna Carta has been the foundation for numerous laws that enshrine the protection of ordinary people around the world and no more so than in the United States of America.

The concept of "due process of law" in Magna Carta was embraced by the leaders of the American Revolution and is embedded in the supremacy clause of the United States Constitution and enforced by the Supreme Court.

King John and one of the barons agreeing to Magna Carta even features on the bronze doors of the US Supreme Court.

The American embroidery panel features John Cabot who discovered parts of America in 1497 for the British. The Pilgrim Fathers are pictured on the left, who settled on the East Coast in 1620. In the centre John Smith is being captured by Chief Powhatan in 1607. Smith was a pioneer and settler who established the first English colony.

The Boston Tea Party 1773 is on the right, with wonderful detail of tea chests being thrown over the side of the ship. Bottom left is General Cornwallis surrendering to George Washington and Washington on his horse as first President. On the right is the iconic home of the President, the White House. The two flags are pre and post-independence.

Magna Carta is mentioned in the American Constitution and is of great historical importance to the country, and unlike the UK, is taught in all American schools.

AMERICA

John Cabot discovered America 1497

Pilgrim Fathers 1620

John Smith captured in Jamestown by Chief Powhatan 1607

Boston Tea Party 1773

General Cornwallis surrenders to George Washington 1776

George Washington First President of the United States

American War of Independence 1776

THE INDIA PANEL

India was the bedrock of the British Empire and our influence in the sub-continent spread far and wide and remains to this day.

The India panel features the Battle of Plassey in 1757, which is when India was colonised by incoming British troops. On the panel you can see Clive of India negotiating with the Mongols after their defeat.

On the left you can see the establishment of the British Raj which ruled India from 1858 to 1947 (the word Raj is the Hindu word for rule).

To its left is a beautiful ceremonial Indian elephant and at the bottom is the logo of the East India Company, which rose to account for half the world's trade and was key to Britain's international dominance in industry and trade throughout this period.

The panel would not be complete of course without Mahatma Ghandi, the father of Indian independence movement. Mahatma in Sanskrit means high souled and venerable and was first given to him as a name in 1914. At the bottom right is the Indian Parliament established in 1947 when India gained Independence from Great Britain.

INDIA

Clive of India - Battle of Plassey 1757

Independence from Great Britain 1947

THE SOUTH AFRICA PANEL

Like the other commonwealth countries, the South African panel depicts key events in South African history, whose legal system was influenced by Magna Carta.

The panel features General Lord Charles Henry Somerset, a British soldier, politician and colonial administrator. He was governor of the Cape Colony of South Africa from 1814 to 1826.

A soldier fighting a Zulu - you can see the extreme contrast of the two different protagonists of the soldier in his uniform and the Zulu with different weapons, a stark display of the clash of two cultures. Zulu War, 1878 to 1879, was fought between the British and the Zulus.

King Cetewayo, the King of the Zulus famously led the Zulu nation to victory against the British in the Battle of Isandlwana.

Boer War, 1899 to 1902, the Second Boer War between Britain and South African Republic and Orange Free State. The war ended in victory for Britain and the annexation of both republics.

Nelson Mandela - surely the most famous South African of all time, a man who truly embodied the principles of freedom, democracy and equality, whose unceasing struggle led to the end of apartheid and saw him become President of South Africa from 1994 to 1999.

Also on the panel is embroidery of Table Mountain and Table Bay - Cape Town's most famous landmark and the South African Parliament Building which houses the modern Parliament.

In 1910 the Union of South Africa was formed.

SOUTH AFRICA

Lord Somerset
Governor to South Africa

King Shaka Zulu
1787 - 1828

Zulu War 1878 - 1879

King Cetewayo
1826 - 1884

Boer War 1899 - 1902

Nelson Mandela

First British Settlers arrive
in Table Bay March 1820

Formation of Union of South Africa 1910

THE AUSTRALIA PANEL

The Australia panel tells the story of how the abiding principles of Magna Carta influenced and are the basis of common law including Australia. To this day, Australians quote Magna Carta when representing themselves in court.

Australia is one of only two countries outside of the UK to own a copy of Magna Carta, purchased from the King's School in Somerset in 1952 for £12,500, it is now priceless and on permanent display in Parliament House, Canberra.

Throughout the embroidery, you can see the native animals of the continent, including koalas, wallabies, kangaroos and emus.

The panel features the Australian and Aboriginal flags. The Aboriginal flag was designed as a symbol of unity and national identity during the land rights movement of the early 1970s.

Overlooking the panel is Captain Cook who arrived on the HMS Endeavour in 1770.

In 1788 the first 736 prisoners arrived in the 'land down under', when Australia became a penal colony until 1823.

You can see world famous Uluru (Ayers Rock) – the sacred site of the Aboriginal people of the area.

An Aborigine playing a didgeridoo represents the indigenous population, who are thought to have been in Australia for up to 80,000 years before it was colonised.

Also on the panel is the Commonwealth Coat of Arms, which is the formal symbol of the Commonwealth of Australia, and the Parliament Building.

AUSTRALIA

Captain James Cook
landed at Botany Bay
28 April 1770

Uluru/Ayres Rock

ADVANCE AUSTRALIA

The Federation of Australia -1st January 1901

THE CANADA PANEL

The Canada panel features the Marquis de Montcalm surrendering to General James Wolfe at the Battle of Quebec.

The panel also features the Canadian wilderness and the broad range of wildlife that lives there, from bears to wolves, moose to beavers. There are also images of the settlers making friends with the local native population, as well as their respective ways of living. The Canadian panel also features lots of 3D features, to help this panel really come alive. From the fur on the bear, to the grass and the clothes on the settlers as well as the indigenous population.

The panel also features the Hudson's Bay Company's crest, which was for a time the de facto government in Canada, and Major General James Wolfe, who was a master military tactician of his time.

CANADA

Battle of Quebec 1759

Major General James Wolfe

Louis Joseph

Marquis de Montcalm

HUDSON'S BAY CO.

ACKNOWLEDGEMENTS

I am extremely grateful to our sponsors, Hart Brown Solicitors who are based in Guildford and also for all the generous support we have received from the various members of Surrey County Council who have donated money to this project and without whom this book could not have been published.

I would also like to thank Runnymede Borough Council for generously paying for the framing of the embroideries, and Lyn Hall for framing them. I would also like to thank Bury St Edmunds Magna Carta Trust for their endless support, especially the wonderful Margaret Charlesworth whose support and encouragement from the start is most appreciated.

I would also like to thank Caroline Ratner for all her hard work in promoting The Magna Carta Embroideries around the UK and the commonwealth countries, Jenny Wilkinson, who took all the wonderful embroidery photographs, Derek J Taylor, the historian and author of the book 'Magna Carta in 20 Places' who very kindly contributed words about the history of Magna Carta. Lindsay Graham, who helped with all the administration of the project, Karen Howieson, who designed the logo and book, and finally to Adrian Keeling, for helping me cart the display easels and embroideries around locally.

HART BROWN SOLICITORS

At first glance, it may not seem an obvious choice for a law firm to support an embroidery project. The creative world of Rhoda Nevins, member of the Royal School of Needlework may seem a long way removed from that of Surrey law firm Hart Brown. However, when the solicitors were introduced to Rhoda's work and heard about the ambitious journey she had embarked upon, to tell the story of Magna Carta through twelve fine embroidery panels, there was no doubt that the firm should support this important work.

The work involved in The Magna Carta Embroidery has taken three years to reach completion. You will learn through this book of the understanding required to undertake this project as well as the passion and dedication of the team. Hart Brown, established in 1919, attribute its own success to its teams continued understanding of the law and by being straightforward and professional in how they work and communicate. The approach is not dissimilar to that of Rhoda and her team of embroiderers.

This is why, when presented with an opportunity to help bring The Magna Carta Embroidery and accompanying book to a wider audience, so that many more people could learn about the origins of the legal world and about how this story is being told through Rhoda Nevins embroidery as well as enjoy the artistry involved, Hart Brown were delighted to oblige.

www.hartbrown.co.uk

UNDERSTANDING | STRAIGHTFORWARD | PROFESSIONAL
Cobham - Cranleigh - Godalming - Guildford - Wimbledon Village - Woking

ABOUT THE EMBROIDERERS

Rhoda could not possibly have completed this huge project without the dedicated team of highly skilled volunteer broderers who worked so hard to get the project completed. Without their skill, dedication, creativity and commitment to the project the Magna Carta Embroidery would not have been completed.

Sue Bone

Sue first began her love of embroidering whilst at Peaslake Infant School in Guildford where she had to make an apron. 51 years later she is still going strong and enjoying all aspects of dressmaking and embroidery.

Patricia Hailstone

Patricia first worked with Rhoda on the Guildford Embroidery and spent two months embroidering the words onto the Guildford piece. This led to Rhoda asking her if she would undertake a similar task for the Magna Carta Embroidery and she ended up sewing the captions on all 12 panels which she did alongside fellow broderer Anne-Marie Gates..

Hilda Nethercott

Hilda taught dressmaking in secondary schools and her dressmaking samples, teaching aids and methods of adapting basic blocks for pattern cutting are now in Winchester Museum as many of the techniques are no longer taught.

Carolynn Stephens

Carolynn is a talented broderer and first worked with Rhoda in 2009 when work began on the Guildford Embroidery. As part of her work on the panels, Carolynn is the lady who would go underneath the embroidered frame to pass the needle back up through the silk to the person doing the embroidery.

Mary Byham

Mary has always enjoyed sewing in some form but mainly dressmaking, she also worked with Rhoda on the Guildford Embroidery, which is now on display in G Live Guildford, and then the Magna Carta Embroidery project followed.

Penny Kramer

Penny twice won the Broderers' Livery Company biannual award called the Percy Levy Trophy and loves the challenge of a large embroidery project.

Judy Baldwin

Judy says that her love with needlework began when she was very young and has found working on the Magna Carta project a really interesting learning curve, especially researching the details for the likeness of the main protagonists and their uniforms and outfits.

Masako Newton

Masako is a freelance hand embroiderer who comes from Kobe in Japan. In 2012, she gained the Royal School of Needlework Diploma in Technical Hand Embroidery with distinction and her stump work piece is featured in Mastering the Art of Embroidery by Sophie Long (ISBN: 978-1906417956).

Masako was also part of the team that embroidered the Duchess of Cambridge's wedding dress and the team of broderers for the Guildford Embroidery in 2009.

Jane Swift

Jane taught at Guildford County School for 18 years where she would be asked to take over the textile department, teaching to 'A' level. Jane did a lot of detailed research on the various pieces she contributed, especially the Bury St Edmunds panel.

Anne Marie Gates

Born and raised in Runnymede Anne Marie has been a broderer all of her life and since retirement has fulfilled her dream of having started a Certificate and Diploma Course in Hand Embroidery at the Royal School of Needlework. She also worked on the Guildford Embroidery Project.

Brenda Fox

Brenda is a founder member of the Guildford Branch of the Embroiders Guild and a member of the Wey Valley Workshop. She has exhibited and sold her work at various venues including Guildford House and Osterley House. Brenda also contributed to the Guildford Embroidery now hanging at G Live.

Pat Sheen

Pat learned how to use a needle and thread at a young age as her mother was a dressmaker and tailor. After retirement she joined a 'creative embroidery' class where she honed her lifelong skills and techniques. She has also had samples accepted for exhibitions. Pat also worked on the Guildford Embroidery.